GEOLOGY

Along Going-to-the-Sun Road
Glacier National Park, Montana

GEOLOGY
Along Going-to-the-Sun Road
Glacier National Park, Montana

By Omer B. Raup, Robert L. Earhart,

James W. Whipple, and Paul E. Carrara

Photography by Omer B. Raup
Pen and ink drawings by Arthur L. Isom and Omer B. Raup

Prepared by the U.S. Geological Survey in cooperation with the National Park Service
Published by Glacier Natural History Association

Going-to-the-Sun Road *winds its way down glacially carved mountainsides into yawning valleys below, descending from alpine meadows (foreground) into deep forests. In this view looking north from Logan Pass, the road passes along the Garden Wall (far right), skirts Haystack Butte (right center), and drops into the valley of McDonald Creek. The steep shoulder of Mount Oberlin is at the far left.*

Library of Congress Catalog Card Number: 82-84746

ISBN 978-0-9343188-11-2

Publishing Consultant: Falcon Press Publishing Co., Inc., Helena, Montana. Bill Schneider, Publisher; Al Abramson, Designer; Sanna Porte, Editor.

Cover photo: Garden Wall and Haystack Butte from MacDonald Creek Valley.

Printed in Canada

PREFACE

Glacier National Park was first studied geologically by Bailey Willis of the U.S. Geological Survey in 1902 as part of a reconnaissance along the 49th parallel. Willis's work formed the foundation for subsequent studies by several geologists. Alden and Stebinger first published on the glacial geology in 1913, and Campbell wrote the first popular geologic account in 1914. Fenton and Fenton in 1931 and Ross in 1959, all of the U.S. Geological Survey, subsequently published technical reports on the Park geology.

Between 1979 and 1985, the U.S. Geological Survey conducted a detailed study of many aspects of the Park geology not previously considered. In cooperation with the National Park Service, this research updates our knowledge of the geology to the current level of the science. This guide discusses the results of these studies along Going-to-the-Sun Road.

The authors gratefully acknowledge the many Glacier Park personnel who have assisted in the planning and who provided logistical support. We especially thank Robert C. Haraden and Phillip R. Iverson, former Superintendents; Clyde M. Lockwood, Chief of Interpretation; and Edwin L. Rothfuss, former Chief of Interpretation. Finally, we wish to thank the countless number of individuals who have reviewed this guide through its various stages of preparation.

February, 1986
Denver, Colorado

O. B. Raup
R. L. Earhart
J. W. Whipple
P. E. Carrara

FOREWORD

Glacier National Park was named for its glacial scenery. The relentless force of huge Ice Age glaciers profoundly altered this landscape, carving the broad U-shaped valleys, knife-edged arêtes, and horn-shaped peaks of the park. No remnant of Pleistocene ice remains, but 50 small alpine glaciers persist to remind us of a time when winters were long and summers short.

Glaciation is only the most recent chapter of Glacier's geologic history. Stories of ancient oceans, mountain building, and fossil life forms lie written in the rock, easily visible along the Going-to-the-Sun Road.

In language intelligible to the lay reader and interesting to the scientist, this geology guide to the road answers some of the questions most asked by Park visitors, such as: How did the rocks get their colors? How have the mountains been shaped? How old are the mountains? How old are the rocks? Answers to these questions are told at the 21 geologic stops included in the guide. The three-dimensional effect of the geologic map included with this guide takes much of the pain out of map reading.

Join authors Raup, Earhart, Whipple, and Carrara for a 36-mile adventure and learn how the rocks were formed, what role the glaciers played in shaping the landscape, and what geological processes are operating today in Glacier Park.

I hope you enjoy your stay in the Park, and that, with the help of this guide, you will leave with a better understanding of its geologic history.

Cindy Nielsen
Chief of Interpretation
Glacier National Park, Montana

CONTENTS

INTRODUCTION

This guide to the geology along Going-to-the-Sun Road in Glacier National Park describes many of the major geologic features of the Park. It is directed toward the Park visitor with little or no background in geology and is intended to contribute to the visitor's appreciation of the natural history of this scenic and geologically outstanding area.

Geology

Most people think of geology as a study of Earth-shaping events that took place millions of years ago. Geologic events did happen in the dim past, but they are also happening today. Volcanoes, for instance, have erupted since the earliest times of the Earth's history, and the eruptions of Mount St. Helens are still fresh in our memories. Geology includes a wide range of processes, such as weathering of rocks; transport of sediments by wind and water; deposition of sediments in lakes and seas; Earth-shaking forces that build mountains; and sculpturing of the land by glaciers, streams, and pounding surf. Clues to these geologic events that happened in the distant past are contained in the rocks.

The three major types of rocks that make up the Earth's crust—*igneous, sedimentary,* and *metamorphic*—result from different geologic processes. *Igneous* rocks form when minerals crystallize from molten magma far below the surface of the Earth, or when hot lavas erupt at the surface. Some examples are granite, diorite, and basalt. *Sedimentary*

GEOLOGIC TIME SCALE

EON	ERA	PERIOD	MILLIONS OF YEARS BEFORE PRESENT	MAJOR EVENTS IN THE GEOLOGIC HISTORY OF GLACIER NATIONAL PARK
Phanerozoic	Cenozoic	Quaternary	2	} Last Ice Age
		Tertiary	63	
	Mesozoic	Cretaceous	138	Collision of crustal plates that caused the folding and faulting that formed the mountains of the Park.
		Jurassic	205	
		Triassic	240	
	Paleozoic	Permian	290	
		Pennsylvanian	330	
		Mississippian	360	Rocks deposited during this time span were removed by erosion
		Devonian	410	
		Silurian	435	
		Ordovician	500	
		Cambrian	570	
Proterozoic	Late		800	—Intrusion of igneous rocks.
	Middle		1600	Deposition of the sedimentary rocks and lavas preserved throughout most of the Park.
	Early		2500	
Archean	Late		3000	
	Middle		3400	
	Early		3800	
	pre-Archean		4550	

rocks form when sediments or chemicals deposited in seas, lakes, streams, or beaches, etc. harden into rock. Sandstone, shale, and limestone are examples. *Metamorphic* rocks are products of change brought about by heat and pressure acting on preexisting igneous or sedimentary rocks within the Earth's crust. Examples are shale converted to slate and limestone to marble.

Geologic time

Geologic processes have been operating since the Earth's formation approximately 4.5 billion years ago. To keep track of the sequence of events through geologic time, geologists have devised a *geologic time scale.* This time scale is used much as the rest of us use a calendar to keep track of daily, monthly, and yearly events. The geologic time scale in simplified form is shown on page 8. The major divisions of time, called *eons,* are in the left column. Smaller divisions of time—*eras* and *periods,* are in the next two columns. The millions of years before the present are to the right.

During the vast Proterozoic Eon, only simple forms of plant life and a few forms of shell-less animals lived in the sea. At the beginning of the Paleozoic Era, 570 million years ago, shell-bearing animals appeared in the sea. Fishes appeared in the Silurian Period, developed rapidly in the Devonian, and have flourished to the present. Amphibians appeared in the Devonian Period, followed by reptiles in the Pennsylvanian. The Mesozoic Era was the "Age of Dinosaurs," the last of whose numbers became extinct at the end of the Cretaceous Period. Small mammals and birds appeared in the Jurassic, long before the dinosaurs died out, but the ancestors of man appeared only about 3.5 million years ago.

It is easy to talk about events that happened hundreds of millions of years ago, but it is very difficult to grasp the immense amounts of time involved. Let's imagine that all of geologic time, from the formation of the Earth to the present, is *one calendar year.* When in that year would various geological events have happened? How do fairly recent events fit into such a time scale? The following table compares the two time scales:

GEOLOGIC TIME AND EVENTS REDUCED TO CALENDAR YEAR

Geologic Time*	Geologic or Historic Event	Calendar Year
4,500 *million years.*	Formation of Earth.	January 1.
1,600—800 m.y.	Deposition of sedimentary rocks preserved throughout Glacier National Park.	August 23-October 27.
570 m.y.	First shell-bearing animals in the sea.	November 16.
420 m.y.	Fish appeared.	November 28.
240—63 m.y.	Age of dinosaurs.	December 12-27.
170—60 m.y.	Collision of crustal plates that formed the mountains of Glacier National Park.	December 17-25.
3.5 m.y.	Ancestors of man.	December 31 5:00 p.m.
20,000 *years.*	Last Ice Age.	December 31 11:58 p.m.
2,000 years.	Birth of Christ.	December 31 11:59:46 p.m.
300 years.	Modern technology.	December 31 Last 2 seconds.

*Time before present.

Names of Rock Formations

Below are the names of the rock formations that you will see during your geological tour of Glacier National Park. The name *Helena* is new to the area and in part replaces the historical name *Siyeh*. To avoid confusion, this historical name, used in older literature about the Park, is given in parentheses. See the *Appendix* for further explanation and for information on the composition of these rock formations.

Geologist's hammer.

Altyn Formation

Appekunny Formation

Empire Formation

Grinnell Formation

Helena (Siyeh) Formation

Prichard Formation

Shepard Formation

Snowslip Formation

The illustration below and the foldout map show the distribution of these rock formations.

Geologic Cross Section.

This simplified geologic cross section crosses the Park in a straight line southwest to northeast. Going-to-the-Sun Road follows the line of section only in a general way, but the section portrays the structural setting of formations as they are seen along the road.

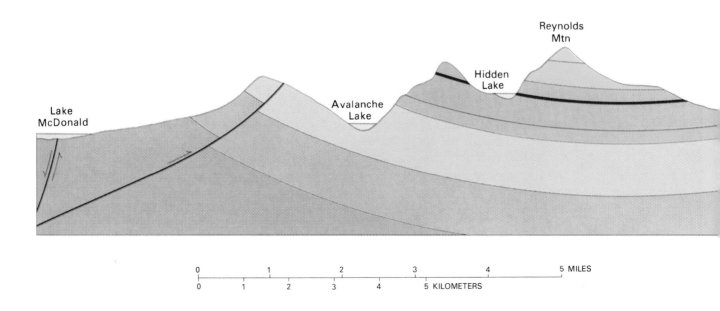

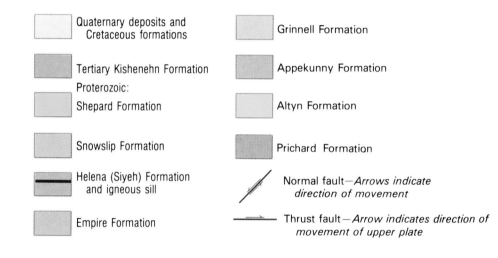

Quaternary deposits and
Cretaceous formations

Tertiary Kishenehn Formation

Proterozoic:

Shepard Formation

Snowslip Formation

Helena (Siyeh) Formation
and igneous sill

Empire Formation

Grinnell Formation

Appekunny Formation

Altyn Formation

Prichard Formation

Normal fault—*Arrows indicate
direction of movement*

Thrust fault—*Arrow indicates direction of
movement of upper plate*

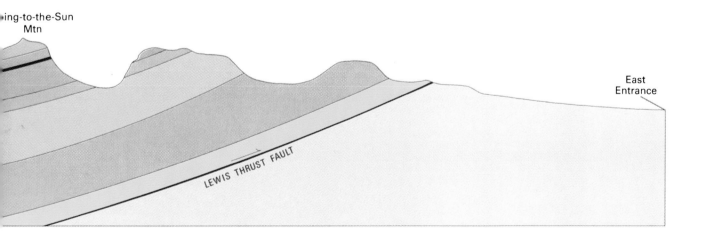

ing-to-the-Sun
Mtn

East
Entrance

LEWIS THRUST FAULT

Some Notes About the Trip

This geologic guide contains 21 stops selected to introduce you to the wide variety of geologic features in Glacier National Park. Six stops are designated as **optional**. These optional stops allow visitors to study the geology in greater detail, but they are not critical to a general geologic overview.

A tour of the 15 major stops takes about 5 hours and 15 minutes, assuming 15 minutes per stop and 1.5 hours of driving time. Distance between Stops 1 and 21 is 35.8 miles (57.6 km).

Eastbound travelers should follow the directions listed in blue in the upper left corner of each page describing a new stop. Westbound travelers should follow directions listed in red in the upper right corner of the same pages. Distances to the next stop are included as are distances from the east entrance station at St. Mary and the west entrance station south of Apgar. You may use either your odometer to calculate point to point distance or your trip mileage recorder if your vehicle is so equipped.

The geologic features are best viewed by beginning the trip from St. Mary, westbound, in the early to mid-morning hours. The trip is also easy to follow from west to east by starting with Stop 21. A partial trip, between Logan Pass and St. Mary on the east side, or between Logan Pass and Lake McDonald on the west side, provides a general geologic overview. However, because of the variety of geologic features on both sides of the Park, taking the entire trip will give you a greater appreciation of the Park's magnificent geology.

The foldout geologic map of the area along and adjacent to the Going-to-the-Sun Road is included in this book. This oblique shaded-relief diagram depicts the landscape as well as the distribution of the rock formations and faults. It also shows the locations of geologic stops along the road. Referring to the map at the various stops will help you understand and appreciate the dimension and distribution of the geologic features. Binoculars are helpful for viewing some of the features far from the road.

Some sections of the Going-to-the-Sun Road are very narrow, especially west of Logan Pass. You are urged to be very cautious of on-coming cars while looking at the rocks in the roadcuts. You are reminded that collecting specimens of rocks, minerals, or plants is prohibited. Please observe this rule. Have a safe and enjoyable trip.

Mountain Goat.

Eastbound Travelers
Distance from West Entrance to this stop
45.6 miles (73 km)

This stop completes your Geology Tour.

Westbound Travelers
Distance from St. Mary Entrance to this stop
3.9 miles (6.2 km)

Next stop: Altyn Formation
2.4 miles (3.8 km) west

Triple Divide Peak Exhibit

This stop is at the National Park Service exhibit called Triple Divide Peak. Park your car on the side of the road by St. Mary Lake (see foldout map).

You are beginning a geologic tour through one of our most beautiful national parks. Geologic events recorded in the rocks and landforms in this Park span a vast amount of time—from the deposition of sedimentary rocks over 1 *billion* years ago; through the mountain building events about 100 *million* years ago; to the sculpturing of mountains by huge glaciers as recently as 20 *thousand* years ago; and to the erosion by stream, wind, and ice that is continuing *today*.

The geologic story of Glacier Park is a saga

Curly Bear Mountain and the other mountains of the Park owe their internal structure to stresses in the Earth's crust caused by the collision of crustal plates and the resulting deformation of the rocks about 100 million years ago.

of ongoing processes and events that started during the early history of the Earth. The story unfolds in the framework of geologic time, a time frame so vast and extensive it is difficult to comprehend. The geologic time scale on page 8 will help you keep track of these events. Technical terms not explained in the text are defined in the Glossary. The Brief Geologic History in the Appendix is also helpful.

Most rocks in Glacier National Park are sedimentary formations of Proterozoic age that were deposited in an ancient sea 1,600 to 800 million years ago. Had you been present during any part of that time, you would have been awed by the stark monotony of the apparently lifeless sea and shore. A closer look, however, would have revealed colonies of very simple plants similar to present-day algae living in the shallow water near the margin of the sea.

The oldest Proterozoic rock unit in this part of the Park is the Altyn Formation. A *rock formation* is a unit of rock that can be identified and distinguished from other units of rock on the basis of its composition, color, age, or other geological features. The Altyn

Formation consists of light tan dolomite and limestone that form cliffs near the bases of Curly Bear Mountain—across the lake—and Singleshot Mountain— opposite Curly Bear.

The Altyn Formation is overlain by the Appekunny Formation, mostly greenish-gray rocks that have interbedded thin white layers of quartzite. Red Eagle Mountain (see the photo on page 15), to the right of Curly Bear, mostly consists of the Appekunny Formation, with the Altyn at its base and the overlying bright red Grinnell Formation at the top. You will get a closer look at these rocks and find out more about them at other stops as you travel up the road.

The Proterozoic sedimentary rocks rest on a major geologic feature called the Lewis thrust fault (see cross section pages 10 and 11). About 100 million years ago, massive segments of the Earth's crust moved eastward from the area of the Pacific Ocean, slammed into the western edge of the North American continent, and forced the rocks to buckle and rise into huge mountain ranges. A similar event is happening today in the Himalaya Mountains, where the

Gleaming layers of white quartzite are interbedded with the greenish gray layers of the Appekunny Formation in the upper part of Singleshot Mountain.

Triple Divide
Peak

Landslide

Red Eagle Mtn

Events span a billion years in the panorama on the southwest side of St. Mary Lake.

subcontinent of India is jamming into Asia. Along the Lewis thrust fault, Proterozoic rocks were shoved eastward about 40 miles (65 km) over much younger rocks of Cretaceous age.

The photograph on page 13 illustrates the magnitude of such forces by showing that the ancient Proterozoic rocks of the Altyn and Appekunny Formations overlie relatively young Cretaceous rocks along the Lewis thrust fault. This relationship is opposite the normal younger-over-older depositional sequence of sedimentary rocks.

The Lewis thrust fault is mostly concealed by loose rubble and landslide deposits, but it is exposed at a few places across the lake near the base of Curly Bear Mountain. The fault appears as a line separating the light tan Altyn Formation from the underlying dark gray shale. At Singleshot Mountain (see photo page 14), the Lewis thrust fault is behind the rubble at the base of the cliff just above the top of the tree line. Light colored layers in the Appekunny Formation are thick beds of quartzite.

The low, tree-covered ridges across the road and across St. Mary Lake are *moraines.* These are composed of glacial debris that was deposited during the retreat of a large glacier that flowed eastward from the head of the St. Mary valley down the valley now occupied by the lake.

The view across St. Mary Lake is a panorama in which events span a billon years. Billion-year-old Proterozoic rocks in Red Eagle Mountain are mostly Appekunny Formation. St. Mary valley and the mountains were carved by glaciers about 20,000 years ago. A *landslide* scarred the flank of Red Eagle Mountain just a few thousand years ago (see photo above).

Eastbound Travelers
Distance from West Entrance to this stop
43.2 miles (69.1 km)

Next stop: Triple Divide Peak Exhibit
2.4 miles (3.8 km) east

Westbound Travelers
Distance from St. Mary Entrance to this stop
6.3 miles (10.1 km)

Next stop: Wild Goose Island Viewpoint
0.3 miles (0.5 km) west

Altyn Formation

This stop is at the parking area at a sharp bend on the south side of the road. Be cautious when turning into this parking area.

Only the upper part of the Altyn Formation, about 1,400 feet (430 m), is present in this part of the Park. The lower part was cut off by the Lewis thrust fault, which is just a few feet below the surface here. Notice on the foldout map that the fault crosses St. Mary Lake just east of this point.

The Altyn Formation was deposited in a

Light-colored, thick-bedded dolomite and limestone of the Altyn Formation at Stop 2.

shallow, warm sea, an environment indicated by the presence of fossil algae called *stromatolites* (see photo below). The present-day relatives of these algae live in

Cross sections of sandy ripple marks.

Fossil algae on weathered limestone surface.

warm seas within the tidal zone and seaward in water less than 100 feet (30 m) deep. Algae require sunlight for survival, so the water had to be shallow enough for sunlight to penetrate to the bottom. Algal life processes aided in precipitating and trapping fine-grained limestone and dolomite. For more information about fossil algae, turn to the Appendix.

such features, follow the trail that starts across the rock wall and goes out to the point toward St. Mary Lake. (The photos on this page were taken on that point.) You can also see many of these sedimentary features in the rocks of the wall itself.

Sandy crosssbedded layers.

Sedimentary features in the Altyn Formation are accentuated by layers and inclusions of sand. The sand was washed into the sea from nearby highlands, and it became interlayered with light-colored limestone and dolomite. Sand now outlines such sedimentary features as *crossbedding* (see photo above) and *ripple marks* (see upper right photo). To see good examples of

Eastbound Travelers
Distance from West Entrance to this stop
42.9 miles (68.6 km)

Next stop: Altyn Formation
0.3 miles (0.5 km) east

Westbound Travelers
Distance from St. Mary Entrance to this stop
6.6 miles (10.6 km)

Next stop: Appekunny Formation
1.5 miles (2.4 km) west

Wild Goose Island Viewpoint

There is parking on both sides of the road at this scenic viewpoint.

This stop provides one of the most beautiful views in the Park. To the west, Mahtotopa, Little Chief, Dusty Star, and Fusillade mountains appear like huge ships steaming into St. Mary Lake. Their sharp prows were sculptured by glaciers. The sides of the "ships" were carved by small glaciers that flowed from the tributary valleys and joined the main glacier that moved down the St. Mary valley between Dusty Star and Fusillade mountains. The main glacier was 2,000 to 3,000 feet (600 to 900 m) thick. The ice rode over the land that you are standing on, but the very tough and resistant carbonate rock of the Altyn Formation resisted the abrasive action of the glacier.

This is a good place to see some of the other rock formations in this part of the Park. To your right, in the bottom half of

Goat Mountain, the greenish gray Appekunny Formation overlies the Altyn. Above the Appekunny is the bright red Grinnell, with the Empire Formation at the top. Mahtotopa Mountain consists mostly of the Grinnell, Empire, and Helena (Siyeh) formations. The Snowslip Formation, which overlies the Helena, comprises the upper parts of Little Chief and Dusty Star mountains, as shown on the foldout map. All these rock formations slope west toward the head of the valley. As you travel up to Logan Pass you will move upward into younger geologic formations.

On your way to Stop 4 you will pass numerous roadcuts in the Appekunny Formation. Although most of the rocks are greenish gray, a few layers are reddish or purplish gray.

Giant monoliths guard jewel-like Wild Goose Island in St. Mary Lake. Vivid colors of the Proterozoic rock formations enhance this view, especially during the morning hours. Geology Stop 4 is around the lake near the base of Goat Mountain.

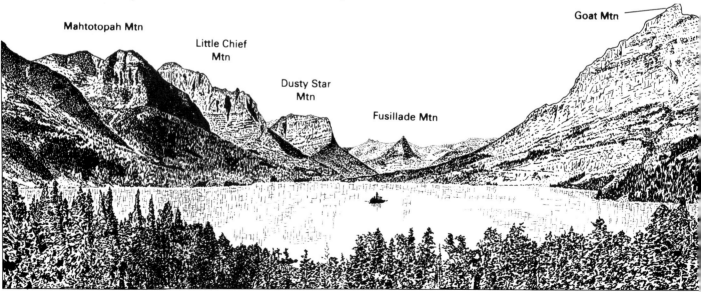

**Stop 3
Geology   18**

Eastbound Travelers
Distance from West Entrance to this stop
41.4 miles (66.2 km)

Next stop: Wild Goose Island Viewpoint
1.5 miles (2.4 km) east

Westbound Travelers
Distance from St. Mary Entrance to this stop
8.1 miles (13 km)

Next stop: Grinnell Formation
3.0 miles (4.8 km) west

Appekunny Formation

This exposure of the Appekunny formation is in a roadcut along the north shore of St. Mary Lake. Large parking areas are on both sides of the road.

The Appekunny Formation at this stop was deposited in deeper water than the underlying Altyn Formation. After the Altyn was deposited, the sea bottom warped downward and the water deepened, possibly by several hundred feet. At the same time, an adjacent rising landmass was shedding vast quantities of fine sediment into the sea. The sea bottom continued to warp downward from the weight of thousands of feet of accumulated sediment. In this part of the Park, the Appekunny Formation is about 2,700 feet (820 m) thick. As the fine silt and clay of the Appekunny

Appekunny Formation at Dead Horse Point.

slowly accumulated, the water became shallower, and conditions were set for deposition of the overlying Grinnell Formation. You will learn more about this at later stops.

This roadcut is in the lower part of the Appekunny Formation. Here, the Appekunny consists mostly of greenish gray siltite and argillite (see Glossary), but elsewhere on the east side of the Park it contains beds of light tan to white quartzite and occasional beds of reddish or purplish gray siltite and argillite.

The Appekunny here contains two types of bedding: *contorted* and *laminated.*

Contorted beds (see photo below), marked by dark green swirls and curved layering, occur in large blocks of siltite near the road and in the massive outcrops at the west end of the roadcut (to the left as you face the roadcut). Rapid deposition of thick layers of sediment on top of very soft, water-saturated mud caused the thick layers to sink into and deform the underlying material.

Laminated beds.

Contorted beds.

The *laminated* beds (see upper right photo), which make up most of the roadcut, originated as fine-grained sediment that accumulated slowly in very quiet, perhaps fairly deep water. Oxygen was depleted from the water to the extent that the iron-bearing minerals in the sediments were chemically *reduced.* Later, when these rocks were recrystallized by heat and pressure, much of the iron-bearing material was converted to the green mineral *chlorite,* which gives the rocks their greenish tint.

There is a great view of St. Mary Lake and the surrounding mountains from the parking area nearest the lake. The large

mountain across the lake is Red Eagle. Continuing to the right are Mahtotopa and Little Chief. Between the mountains are *hanging valleys,* which formed at the junction of different-sized glaciers. The large, vigorous glacier that carved St. Mary valley scoured its bed more deeply than did its smaller tributary glaciers, thus leaving hanging tributary valleys after the glaciers receded (see page 21). You will see many hanging valleys, and waterfalls spilling from them, as you travel through the Park.

High on the side of Little Chief Mountain is a dark band of rock between lighter-colored rocks. The dark band is an igneous *sill* that was intruded as very hot molten material between the sedimentary layers. Carbonate rocks immediately above and below the sill were bleached by the heat. You will read more about this sill later.

On leaving Stop 4, you pass more outcrops of the Appekunny Formation. The contact between the Appekunny and the overlying Grinnell Formation is near the turnoff to Going-to-the-Sun Point. Beyond this contact, the Grinnell Formation is mostly red, but it contains a few green layers. About two miles (3.2 km) after you leave Stop 4, you will pass Sunrift Gorge, where the brightly colored Grinnell Formation is deeply incised by Baring Creek.

Sunrift Gorge, as seen from the trail that goes up from the road, is eroded straight as an arrow about 1,000 feet (300 m) along a vertical fault that shattered the rocks along this line. Baring Creek found easier cutting through here than through the tougher rock on either side. The creek leaves the fault zone at a right-angle turn at the observation point.

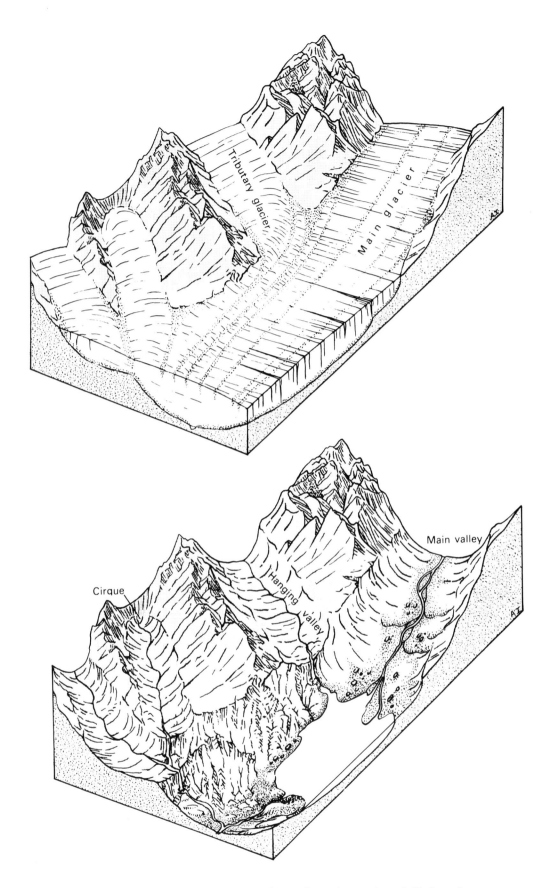

Formation of a hanging valley. *The main glacier and its tributaries cut broad U-shaped valleys through the Proterozoic terrane. Streams tumble from the tributary valleys that were left "hanging" above the main valley after the ice melted away.*

Eastbound Travelers
Distance from West Entrance to this stop
38.4 miles (61.4 km)

Next stop: Appekunny Formation
3.0 miles (4.8 km) east

Westbound Travelers
Distance from St. Mary Entrance to this stop
11.1 miles (17.8 km)

Next stop: Jackson Glacier Exhibit
1.9 miles (3 km) west

Grinnell Formation

This roadcut exposure of the red Grinnell Formation is near the St. Mary Falls trailhead. The small parking area is on the south side of the road opposite the outcrop.

The bright red Grinnell Formation is one of the most colorful and easily recognizable rock units in Glacier Park. The Grinnell Formation was named after Grinnell Mountain, which honors George Bird Grinnell, an enthusiastic promoter of the Park and a well-known American writer.

The Grinnell Formation accumulated through continued deposition of silt and clay above the Appekunny Formation, as shown on the foldout map. Because the water had become very shallow, the Grinnell Formation is interpreted to have been deposited on broad tidal flats. The ebb and flow of the tides worked and reworked the muds washed into the sea by streams from the neighboring highlands.

During very low tides, as vast expanses of the flats dried out, the mud cracked. Some of these cracked surfaces were preserved when they were later covered by more mud.

During occasional storms, swollen streams spread thin sheets of crossbedded sand across the flats. Rapidly moving currents sometimes ripped up flakes of dried mud and redeposited them as jumbled *mudchip breccia.*

At other times, gentler waves and currents produced wavy surfaces called *ripple marks,* now preserved on some rock bedding planes.

The bright red color of these rocks is due to the oxidation state of iron-bearing minerals. Iron and oxygen from the atmosphere combined in the shallow water or sometimes-dry environment to form the red mineral hematite (Fe_2O_3). As little as three percent hematite in the rock will give it this bright red color. (For more information on rock colors, see the Appendix.)

The formation above the Grinnell is the Empire Formation, but the Empire—mostly green argillite and siltite—is not well exposed along the road on the east side of the Park. In composition, the Empire is *transitional* between the underlying tidal flat deposits of the Grinnell and the overlying deeper water carbonates of the Helena (Siyeh). You will have an opportunity to examine the Empire Formation at Stop 17, west of Logan Pass. The Helena Formation is described at Stop 7.

Virginia Falls, which can be viewed across the valley from the downhill end of the parking area, is a classic example of a waterfall spilling over the lip of a hanging valley. Up to the left, the igneous sill is high on the shoulder of Little Chief Mountain. Farther west the road climbs up to the level of the sill.

The colorful red rocks beside the road in the short ride to Stop 6 are all part of the Grinnell Formation. Notice the narrow green beds interlayered, at places, with the red rocks. These beds indicate slightly deeper water and a fluctuating sea level.

Bright red Grinnell Formation in the roadcut at Stop 5 is shown above. The small fold in the rocks, just below the man in the photo, was formed during the period of thrust faulting. The hammer the man is holding rests on the rock surface showing mudcracks (left photo). Ripple marks are preserved in the rocks just to the right of the man's feet (below). Mudchip breccia in white quartzite (lower left photo) is in the white area at the left side of the above photo.

Reminder: Collecting rock samples is prohibited in the Park. Please leave them for others to enjoy.

Eastbound Travelers
Distance from West Entrance to this stop
36.5 miles (58.4 km)

Next stop: Grinnell Formation
1.9 miles (3 km) east

Westbound Travelers
Distance from St. Mary Entrance to this stop
13 miles (20.8 km)

Next stop: Reynolds Creek Viewpoint
and Helena Formation
3.8 miles (6.1 km) west

Jackson Glacier Exhibit

This stop is at the viewpoint and National Park Service exhibits for Jackson Glacier.

Jackson Glacier, which is about 5.5 miles (8.8 km) from this viewpoint, rests on a 15-degree dip bedrock slope of the Helena (Siyeh) Formation. Like most of the glaciers in the Park, Jackson Glacier was much larger during the middle of the 19th

Jackson Glacier.

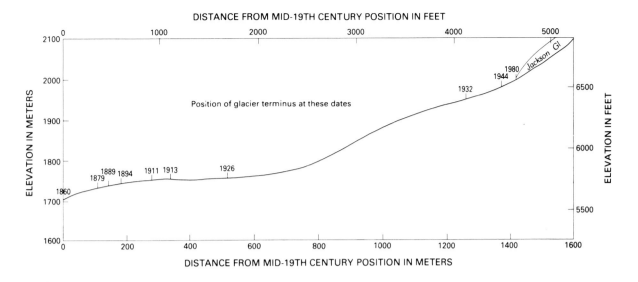

This diagram illustrates the recession of Jackson Glacier from its mid-19th century position.

century, when it and Blackfoot Glacier to the east were one continuous ice body. Together they had a total surface area of more than three square miles (7.8 km²). At that time, a tongue of Jackson Glacier extended beyond the steep bedrock dip slope and into the forest below. The ice's present position is a result of glacial retreat that started about 1860, as indicated by the age of the oldest trees now growing in the area once occupied by ice.

Retreat rates appear to have been relatively slow, less than 25 feet per year (seven m/year) until about 1910, when they seem to have increased. Once the glacier had retreated to the bedrock slope, during the mid to late 1920s, retreat became quite rapid. Not only did the glacier lose mass by melting, but large sections broke off and slid down the bedding surface, which was lubricated by melt water. The period of rapid retreat corresponds to a period of warmer summer temperatures and decreased precipitation in this region. In 1913, Jackson Glacier was reported to have retreated about 1,000 feet (300 m) back from its mid-19th century position. In 1980, the glacier had retreated about 4,800 feet (1,465 m) from its mid-19th century position—a loss of about 76 percent of its former surface area. The

glacier will be short-lived if the present warm and dry climatic trend continues. Even at its mid-19th century extent, Jackson Glacier was small compared to the huge glaciers that sculptured the Park's mountains and valleys. The last of these giants filled the valleys about 20,000 years ago.

Three physical features of Jackson Glacier are shown in the photo. The *bergschrund* is a deep crack or *crevasse* at the head of the glacier that separates the moving ice from the snowfield at the head of the *cirque*. A cirque is a steep-walled, amphitheaterlike hollow carved by a glacier at the head of a valley. This cirque is still occupied by a glacier. Crevasses farther down the glacier are caused by tension owing to different parts of the glacier moving at different speeds. The mid-19th century *moraine* indicates the glacier's maximum extent during its most recent advance.

Many lakes in valleys downstream from active glaciers have a milky blue to milky green color. This color is caused by suspended particles of finely ground rock powder called *glacial flour*, which is produced when rocks embedded at the base of a glacier abrade the underlying rocks.

As you approach Stop 7, you will round the shoulder of Piegan Mountain (see foldout map), where you have a magnificent view of Heavy Runner Mountain across the valley and a beautiful hanging valley to the right. Majestic, pyramid-shaped Reynolds Mountain towers above (see illustration below). Alpine peaks such as Reynolds Mountain are called *horns* or *matterhorns*. You'll read more about them at Logan Pass, Stop 10.

The waterfalls next to the road at each end of the tunnel are fed by springs high on the mountainside. You'll learn more about these at Logan Pass, too.

A valley perched over a valley. Panorama from Going-to-the-Sun Road east of Piegan Mountain Tunnel.

Eastbound Travelers
Distance from West Entrance to this stop
32.7 miles (52.3 km)

Next stop: Jackson Glacier Exhibit
3.8 miles (6.1 km) east

Westbound Travelers
Distance from St. Mary Entrance to this stop
16.8 miles (26.9 km)

Next stop: Fossil Algae, Helena
(Siyeh) Formation
0.4 miles (0.6 km) west

Reynolds Creek Viewpoint and Helena (Siyeh) Formation

This viewpoint is just west of the Eastside Tunnel on the downhill side of the road (see foldout map).

Few visitors to the Park are unmoved by this view. Breath-taking heights, dramatic peaks, and plummeting waterfalls all result from the erosive power of mighty glaciers that filled these valleys as recently as 20,000 years ago, a time well within the history of modern man's ancestors. Climatic conditions then were similar to those today in central Alaska, where whole mountain ranges are in the icy grip of huge glaciers.

At this vantage point, near Logan Pass, the Park's upper formations—the Helena (Siyeh), Snowslip, and Shepard—come into view. The rocks in the roadcut are dolomite and limestone ledges of the Helena Formation. The Helena extends about 8 miles along the road in a westerly direction nearly to The Loop. You will see much of the Helena as you travel along the road and at later stops.

The Helena Formation was deposited in fairly shallow water during a time when relatively minor amounts of mud and silt were being carried into the sea. Limestone and dolomite were chemically precipitated from the seawater, a process aided by the algae that lived in the warm water. Thin to thick beds of gray dolomite and limestone in the Helena characteristically weather to a buff color owing to very small amounts of iron. (See explanation of rock colors in the Appendix.)

The rocks above the Helena are of the Snowslip Formation, which consists mostly of red to green argillite and siltite but also contains many layers of quartzite, silty dolomite, and limestone. This formation makes up the lower three-quarters of Clements Mountain. It was deposited during a return to very shallow water conditions accompanied by a greater influx of sand and silt from the adjacent landmass. You will learn more about the Snowslip at Stop 13 near The Loop, where you can examine it more closely.

The tops of Clements and Reynolds Mountains are composed of the Shepard Formation (see foldout map), mostly dolomite and limestone with abundant fossil algae deposited in an environment similar to that of the Helena Formation. The Shepard is the youngest Proterozoic formation visible from Going-to-the-Sun Road.

The upper part of the Helena contains two distinctive layers, a *fossil algae zone* and a dark *sill* of intruded igneous rock called *diorite*. Look below and to the left of the road and see where the upper part of the sill interfingers into the Helena Formation. This sill is the same one you saw at a distance on Little Chief Mountain. The next two stops will give you a chance to inspect these interesting rocks more closely.

Layers of dense, gray dolomite in the Helena Formation make resistant steps where cascading waterfalls tumble down the mountainsides. You will see many scenic examples of this between this stop and The Loop. When you proceed toward Stop 8, notice the stairstep falls as you pass Lunch Creek.

Near Logan Pass, the upper rock formations of the Park come into view. The Visitors Center on Logan Pass is perched at the head of Reynolds Creek Valley where ice fields once fed glaciers that flowed north and south from the pass. Telephoto view shows an igneous sill intruding the Helena (Siyeh) Formation.

Eastbound Travelers
Distance from West Entrance to this stop
32.3 miles (51.7 km)

Next stop: Reynolds Creek Viewpoint and
Helena (Siyeh) Formation
0.4 miles (0.6 km) east

Westbound Travelers
Distance from St. Mary Entrance to this stop
17.2 miles (27.5 km)

Next stop: Igneous Sill
0.3 miles (0.5 km) west

Fossil Algae, Helena (Siyeh) Formation

This stop is uphill and across the road from the parking area at Lunch Creek.

Look across the road at the rocks shown in the photo below. This outcrop of the algal zone, which is about 100 feet (30 m) thick, extends up the road to the left and around the curve for a few hundred feet. Take a few minutes to walk along these roadcuts where the algae contain many different forms.

Fossilized algae *that lived in a warm, shallow sea more than a billion years ago are preserved in the Helena (Siyeh) Formation.*

The algae grew in the sea, probably many miles from shore but in water depths from the tidal zone to as much as 100 feet (30 m). The water had to be fairly shallow and nearly free of suspended sediment because the algae needed sunlight to live. The environment probably was much like that at the present time around the Florida Keys and the Bahama Islands. Most of the rock consists of calcium carbonate (limestone) precipitated by chemical processes associated with the algae's life cycle.

The fossil algae (stromatolites) take many forms (see photo below). Some individual algal heads resemble cabbages; others are stacked in single or branching columns. Each form was a colony of algae.

Various forms of stromatolites in fossil algae zone.

A distinctive form, *Conophyton* (see photo below)—so named because it resembles columns of stacked cones—is unique to this zone. It generally grew as groups of nested cones near the middle of these stromatolite beds. This sequence of stromatolite beds, collectively referred to as the Conophyton

Closeup view of Conophyton.

zone, is in the same general position in the Helena Formation throughout the Park. As such, it is a distinctive "marker bed" and is a great aid in mapping the geology of the Park. For more information about fossil algae, see the Fossil Algae section in the Appendix.

There are many thin beds of stromatolites throughout the Helena Formation. You may see some of these in the area of Logan Pass.

Fossil algae.

From this stop, look back at the dramatic view down St. Mary valley. Notice that its profile has the characteristic U-shape of valleys eroded by large glaciers. Valleys that have been eroded primarily by streams have a V-shaped profile. You will learn more about valley erosion at later stops.

Eastbound Travelers
Distance from West Entrance to this stop
32 miles (51.2 km)

Westbound Travelers
Distance from St. Mary Entrance to this stop
17.5 miles (28 km)

Next stop: Fossil Algae, Helena
(Siyeh) Formation
0.3 miles (0.5 km) east

Next stop: Logan Pass
0.3 miles (0.5 km) west

Igneous Sill

Optional

This optional stop is at a curve in the road halfway between stops 8 and 10. Park on the south side of the road. A large snowdrift may cover the igneous sill until midsummer.

Although Stop 9 is a great place to see the igneous sill, the stop is *optional,* because Big Drift covers the sill in the early part of the summer. Much of the snow is gone, however, by the first week in August. You have another opportunity to see the sill at Stop 15 (see foldout map).

Look across the road to the left of the snow bank and locate the rocks as pictured below. The dark rock below and to the left of the hammer in the photo is the diorite sill noted earlier (see Glossary). From the left side of the roadcut, the top of the sill follows a bedding surface of the overlying

Hot molten magma injected between sedimentary layers of the Helena (Siyeh) Formation formed a tabular body of igneous rock called diorite.

Igneous sill below road level.

Helena (Siyeh) Formation as far as the hammer. At the hammer, the top of the sill cuts abruptly downward across layers of carbonate rock toward the right side of the roadcut. This illustrates how the very fluid, molten rock moved from one bedding plane to another as it invaded the Helena Formation.

This sill is conspicuous throughout the Park. Most of the rock is medium to fairly coarse grained, but near its borders, where it came in contact with the relatively cool rocks of the Helena Formation, it chilled rapidly and hence is very fine grained. Grain size is coarser near the middle of the sill where the magma crystallized more slowly.

The sill can be seen below road level by walking down the road several yards from the parking area (see photo above).

The age of the sill has not yet been determined, but sills of similar composition in the upper part of the Helena Formation in the Bob Marshall Wilderness south of the Park have been dated at 725 to 775 million years old, as determined by the *radioactive decay* of an *isotope* of potassium (see Glossary).

The contrast between the dark, massive diorite and the lighter sedimentary rock is further enhanced by the bleached and *altered* zone at the contact. The conspicuous light-colored rock above the sill is altered limestone, altered by the intense heat associated with intrusion of the sill. Where the sill is as much as 300 feet (90 m) thick, it baked or bleached the rocks below it as well as those above it. Where heating from the sill was moderate, it removed organic matter and recrystallized the limestone to marble. Where heating was more intense, the carbonate and other minerals in the limestone were recombined into new silicate minerals.

As you leave this stop and head for Logan Pass and the Continental Divide, you will pass exposures of the upper part of the Helena Formation.

Eastbound Travelers
Distance from West Entrance to this stop
31.7 miles (50.7 km)

Westbound Travelers
Distance from St. Mary Entrance to this stop
17.8 miles (28.5 km)

Next stop: Igneous Sill
0.3 miles (0.5 km) east

Next stop: Garden Wall Viewpoint
0.5 miles (0.8 km) west

Logan Pass

This stop is at the top of the first low ridge west of the Visitor Center. Park in the large parking lot and walk a few paces along the Hidden Lake Nature Trail.

This is the highest stop (elevation 6,646 ft—2,026 m) on your geologic tour through Glacier National Park. You are standing on the Continental Divide (see foldout map). Streams flow west from this pass to the Pacific Ocean and east to the Atlantic by way of Hudson Bay. From this vantage point, you can see the vast open landscape of this beautiful glacially sculptured terrain.

Clements Mountain and Reynolds Mountain (the next high peak to the left) are excellent examples of *horns* or *matterhorns*, sharp pyramidal peaks carved by glaciers from three or more sides. The name

Scattered patches of snow are only reminders of the great ice fields that covered the alpine meadows at Logan Pass 20,000 years ago. Geology Stop 10 is just to the right of the building along the trail to Hidden Lake toward Clements Mountain, the high peak in the photo.

matterhorn comes from the famous mountain in the Pennine Alps. The U-shaped valleys that extend east and west from the pass were eroded by glaciers that originated at the pass. An exhibit in the Visitors Center illustrates how the pass and the adjacent valleys were formed. The Visitors Center, a favorite stop, also features maps, books, and other exhibits on many aspects of the Park's natural and cultural history.

The gray to buff ledges next to the trail are limestone and dolomite in the upper part of the Helena (Siyeh) Formation. Above these is the pale reddish and greenish Snowslip Formation, which extends three-quarters of the way up Clements and Reynolds Mountains. The tops of these mountains are composed of the Shepard Formation. You will have a close view of the Snowslip at Stop 13, but the Shepard does not crop out along the road; the closest view of it is from here.

The prominent mountains to the east Going-to-the-Sun Mountain behind the Visitors Center and Piegan Mountain to the left, are eroded from the Helena and Snowslip Formations (see foldout map). In the afternoon light, the reddish color of the Snowslip contrasts with the grayish tan of the Helena.

Two springs that flow from the middle of Piegan Mountain originate from the melting of Piegan Glacier on the other side of the mountain. Glacial melt water dissolves calcium-bearing rocks from fractures in the Snowslip and Helena Formations, thereby forming channels through the mountain. These springs are the source of the waterfalls you saw at either end of the tunnel.

Glacier lilies.

Bear grass.

Eastbound Travelers
Distance from West Entrance to this stop
31.2 miles (49.9 km)

Next stop: Logan Pass
0.5 miles (0.8 km) east

Westbound Travelers
Distance from St. Mary Entrance to this stop
18.3 miles (29.3 km)

Next stop: Glacial Landscape Exhibit
3.8 miles (6.1 km) west

Garden Wall Viewpoint

This stop is at the parking area near a large curve in the road just west of Logan Pass.

Here, you are standing at the head of a deep U-shaped valley cut by the glacier that flowed from Logan Pass to Lake McDonald and beyond. Mount Oberlin is to the left as you look down the valley. The imposing cliff to the right is the Garden Wall, crowned by the Bishops Cap. The Garden Wall is a mountain landform called an *arête*—a French word meaning "fish bone." This sharp, jagged arête was eroded by

Going-to-the-Sun Road *traverses the Garden Wall and Haystack Butte.*

glaciers cutting into the ridge from opposite sides. It might be hard to believe, but the Garden Wall is even steeper and more precipitous on its other side, where Grinnell Glacier is sheltered by its towering headwall. Grinnell is one of the largest remaining glaciers in the Park.

Going-to-the-Sun Road is etched into the steep slopes of the Garden Wall and Haystack Butte. The Highline Trail, above the road toward the right of the photo on page 35, rewards the hiker with some of the most spectacular alpine scenery in the Park. This popular trail begins at Logan Pass opposite the Visitors Center. Slopes along the trail are carpeted with wildflowers and frequented by bighorn sheep, mountain goats, and marmots. The trail leads to Granite Park chalet, but the ambitious hiker can continue on to Waterton Lake or to Many Glacier, east of the Continental Divide.

As you drive northward down the road, notice that the rocks have been bent into a large downward fold called a *syncline*. It is best seen from 1.2 miles (1.9 km) to 1.4 miles (2.3 km) from this stop, but parking along this stretch of road is limited to three very small areas on the right side.

At Heavens Peak, you can see the layering of the Helena (Siyeh) Formation in the west limb of the syncline, sloping eastward toward the low part of the fold at Glacier Wall. Haystack Butte is a part of the east limb of the syncline, as the layers there dip westward. In addition to its downward bend, the entire syncline tilts or plunges north, away from you. This syncline, illustrated below, formed when the rocks were thrust eastward along the Lewis thrust fault.

As you proceed to Stop 12, you will pass by the Weeping Wall, where springs fed by melting snow high up along the Garden Wall issue water into countless small streams that cascade down the mountainside.

Downwarping of the rocks *is indicated by the opposing inclinations of strata (as shown by the arrows) on Heavens Peak and Haystack Butte. This structure, called a syncline, trends northerly through most of the length of the Park. The axis of the syncline passes through the flat-dipping rocks on Glacier Wall.*

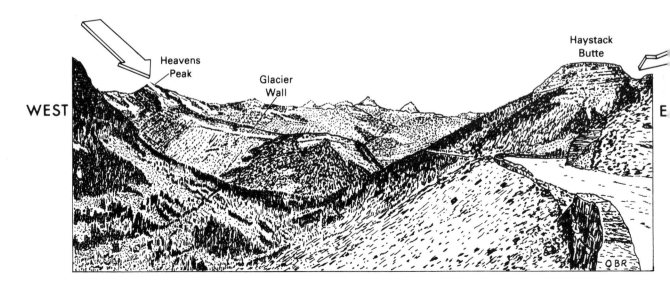

WEST   E

Heavens Peak   Glacier Wall   Haystack Butte

Eastbound Travelers
Distance from West Entrance to this stop
27.4 miles (43.8 km)

Next stop: Garden Wall Viewpoint
3.8 miles (6.1 km) east

Westbound Travelers
Distance from St. Mary Entrance to this stop
22.1 miles (35.4 km)

Next stop: Snowslip Formation
3.7 miles (5.9 km) west

Glacial Landscape Exhibit

This stop is at the National Park Service exhibit called Glacial Landscape. A large parking area is on the west side of the road.

This viewpoint offers a magnificent panorama of the west side of the Park, the most obvious features of which are steep mountains and broad, U-shaped valleys (see illustration below). Prior to glaciation these valleys were V-shaped, narrow, and winding, typical of valleys eroded by streams. McDonald Glacier and its tributaries widened and straightened them and carved out their U-shaped profiles. When the glaciers attained maximum size about 20,000 years ago, they completely

Ice-carved U-shaped valleys, hanging tributaries, and matterhorns dominate the Proterozoic rock landscape along Going-to-the-Sun Road.

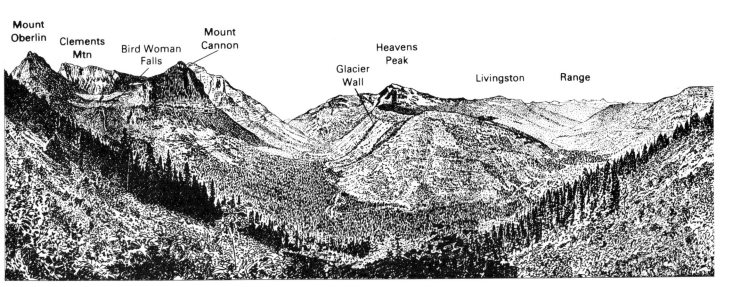

filled the valleys below. The top of the ice was about where you are standing, and it overtopped Glacier Wall.

Bird Woman Falls plummets from a hanging valley where, about 20,000 years ago, a small mountain glacier joined a larger, more deeply eroding glacier that occupied what is now Logan Creek Valley. The moraine in the middle of the hanging valley above Bird Woman Falls was deposited by a small glacier during the middle of the 19th century. According to legend, Bird Woman Falls was so named because the moraine resembles the Bird Woman of local Indian lore (see illustration below).

Notice the numerous snow avalanche tracks on the left side of the main valley, on the right flank of Mount Cannon. Frequent avalanches keep the tracks free of large trees and allow only low and rapidly growing willow and alder shrubs to grow.

Dead trees on the side of Glacier Wall remain from a major forest fire in 1967.

Mount Oberlin and many other pyramidal peaks—matterhorns—owe their distinctive form to the erosive action of glaciers on two or more sides of the peak.

As you drive to Stop 13 you will see many exposures of the Helena (Siyeh) Formation, especially at Bird Woman Falls viewpoint, which is just beyond Haystack Creek.

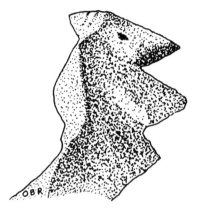

Bird Woman Moraine.

Eastbound Travelers
Distance from West Entrance to this stop
23.7 miles (37.9 km)

Next stop: Glacial Landscape Exhibit
3.7 miles (5.9 km) east

Westbound Travelers
Distance from St. Mary Entrance to this stop
25.8 miles (41.2 km)

Next stop: Oolite Zone, Helena
(Siyeh) Formation
0.2 miles (0.3 km) west

Snowslip Formation

This stop is next to the roadcut, 0.1 miles below the hairpin curve called The Loop.

The Snowslip Formation overlies the Helena (Siyeh) Formation as you saw at Logan Pass, Stop 10. It might seem strange that, though you have come a long way down the road from Logan Pass, you are at the same rock formation that was above you at the pass. The reason is that this stop is near the low part of the syncline (see illustration, page 36). The Snowslip Formation, along with the other

Colorful Snowslip Formation *contains red and green argillite, siltite, and quartzite near The Loop on Going-to-the-Sun Road.*

sedimentary strata, have been bent down to a lower elevation than they are at Logan Pass. (See the foldout map.)

The rocks of the Snowslip Formation were deposited in vast tidal flats much like the rocks of the Grinnell Formation. After the Helena was deposited, the land areas adjacent to the sea were elevated, and streams washed large quantities of fine sediment into the sea. The sea floor sank—or subsided—very slowly, while the accumulation of fine-grained sediment kept pace with this subsidence.

Ripple marks, mudcracks, and mudchip breccia in argillite and sandstone beds.

Thin crossbedded sandstones were deposited by vigorous streams that occasionally carried sand across the mud flats. Sandfilled mudcracks and mudchip breccias (see photo above) indicate that wide expanses of mud sometimes dried and cracked, only to be swept over by storm waves or currents which ripped them up and redeposited them. The wavy surfaces of ripple marks tell of gentle, oscillating wave action or of the ripple effects of currents. Iron-bearing minerals give the Snowslip its pale red to pale green color, varied by

shades of yellow, orange, and light purple. Traces of carbonate minerals give many of these strata a pastel tint.

Stromatolite bed.

The Snowslip contains a few beds of stromatolites, or fossil algae (see photo above). One bed is about 330 feet (120 paces) down the road from the middle of the parking area. The algae had difficulty surviving on the Snowslip tidal flats because they were frequently inundated by mud. Their battle against the mud, however, resulted in very colorful fossils. The pink and green colors are due to iron-bearing minerals present along the laminations and in the argillite around the algal heads. These multicolored stromatolites are characteristic of the Snowslip Formation.

From this stop onward you will progress downward through the sequence of Proterozoic rock formations (see foldout map).

Look across the valley of McDonald Creek to a spectacular view of Heavens Peak. A small glacier and its associated moraine are below the steep face of the peak. Like many of the high-perched moraines in the Park, this moraine probably dates from the mid-19th century, when the Park's glaciers were much larger than they are today.

Eastbound Travelers
Distance from West Entrance to this stop
23.5 miles (37.6 km)

Next stop: Snowslip Formation
0.2 miles (0.3 km) east

Westbound Travelers
Distance from St. Mary Entrance to this stop
26 miles (41.6 km)

Next stop: Igneous Sill
0.4 miles (0.6 km) west

Oolite Zone, Helena (Siyeh) Formation

Optional

The parking area for this optional stop is on the uphill side of the road. The oolite zone starts at the upper end of the parking area and extends up the road for about 475 feet (145 m). Use extreme caution if you walk along this narrow road.

This is an *optional* stop for those interested in some of the details of the depositional features in these sedimentary rocks.

The *oolite* (pronounced *oh eh lite)* beds in this zone are interbedded with layers of argillite. These two rock types can be distinguished easily by their *appearance* and *feel.* The oolite beds are gray and crossbedded, and on weathered surfaces they feel like *coarse sand paper.* The interbedded argillite layers are pale yellow to tan and are *smooth* to the touch.

Oolite is a rock composed of small, spherical-shaped objects that resemble small fish eggs and are called *ooliths.* The ooliths range in size from 0.01 to 0.08 inches (0.25 to 2 mm) but are most commonly 0.02 to 0.04 inches (0.5 to 1 mm). These ooliths are made of calcium carbonate. They have concentric layers commonly enclosing a nucleus, such as a grain of quartz or fragment of limestone or dolomite.

Ooliths form in warm, shallow water in places where calcium carbonate is being deposited. The spherical shapes and concentric layering result from outward growth during constant agitation by waves and currents. Oolite deposits can be seen today on the shores of Great Salt Lake in Utah where they form banks of oolitic sand.

The argillite layers interbedded with the oolite beds were once muds and silts that were deposited periodically over the layers of ooliths.

This oolite zone is in a *transition* between the underlying dolomite and limestone of the main part of the Helena Formation and the argillites and siltites of the overlying Snowslip.

Gritty, gray layers of oolite *are interlayered with tan argillite (upper left). The oolite beds are crossbedded (upper right), and they look and feel like coarse sand paper. Under a 10-power hand lens (lower left), the roundness of the grains and their concentric growth rings are apparent. Under a 30-power microscope (lower right), radial structures can also be seen.*

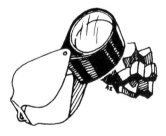

Hand lens.

Eastbound Travelers
Distance from West Entrance to this stop
23.1 miles (37 km)

Next stop: Oolite Zone, Helena
(Siyeh) Formation
0.4 miles (0.6 km) east

Westbound Travelers
Distance from St. Mary Entrance to this stop
26.4 miles (42.2 km)

Next stop: Fossil Algae, Helena
(Siyeh) Formation
0.3 miles (0.5 km) west

Igneous Sill

This stop is 375 feet (114 m) down the road from the lower end of the Westside Tunnel.

The upper part of an igneous sill and the overlying "baked zone" are exposed in the roadcut. This is the same sill viewed at Stop 9 (see foldout map), but only its upper six feet (1.8 m) are exposed here. The very hot molten material came up along fissures from deep in the Earth's crust at temperatures exceeding 1,000 degrees Celsius and, under high pressure, was forcibly injected into the Helena (Siyeh) Formation. The fairly smooth upper surface of the sill where the man in the photo is standing shows that the molten rock was injected along the flat bedding planes of the sedimentary rocks. The upper few feet of the sill is fine grained, because it chilled rapidly when it came in contact with the relatively cool sedimentary rocks. The middle of the sill is much more coarse grained because it cooled more slowly, thus allowing greater time for crystallization of the minerals. These minerals are predominantly hornblende and feldspar, with minor amounts of quartz, mica, and iron oxides. On the basis of its composition and texture, the igneous rock is called *diorite*.

During intrusion the molten rock heated, altered, and bleached the overlying sedimentary rocks. See Stop 9 for more information about the sill.

Diorite, *an igneous rock, was injected as molten magma into the sedimentary rocks of the Helena (Siyeh) Formation.*

Eastbound Travelers
Distance from West Entrance to this stop
22.8 miles (36.5 km)

Next stop: Igneous Sill
0.3 miles (0.5 km) east

Westbound Travelers
Distance from St. Mary Entrance to this stop
26.7 miles (42.7 km)

Next stop: Empire Formation
1.3 miles (2.1 km) west

Fossil Algae, Helena (Siyeh) Formation

Optional

Two narrow parking areas are located about 0.1 miles apart on the downhill side of the road near this optional stop.

The fossil algae at this *optional* stop is in the same stromatolite zone as at Stop 8 east of Logan Pass. Although this outcrop is smaller than the one at Stop 8, it contains excellent examples of algal heads that resemble large cabbages. Other fossil algae here include colonies of small "cabbage heads" stacked in single or branching columns plus stacked inverted cones called *Conophyton*. The *Conophyton zone* of the Helena (Siyeh) Formation, which reaches a thickness of 100 feet (30 m), persists throughout most of Glacier Park. These colonial algae lived in a warm, shallow sea during Proterozoic time. For more information on fossil algae, see the Appendix.

As you drive down the road toward Stop 17, enjoy the spectacular view of Bird Woman Falls ahead, the towering peaks of Mount Oberlin to the left, and Mount Cannon.

*"**Cabbage heads**" and columns of stacked fossil algae cones (stromatolites).*

Stop 16
Geology   44

Eastbound Travelers
Distance from West Entrance to this stop
21.5 miles (34.4 km)

Next stop: Fossil Algae, Helena
(Siyeh) Formation
1.3 miles (2.1 km) east

Westbound Travelers
Distance from St. Mary Entrance to this stop
28 miles (44.8 km)

Next stop: Grinnell Formation
4.6 miles (7.4 km) west

Empire Formation

Optional

This optional stop is on the west side of the road at a curve near where the Going-to-the-Sun Road begins to climb uphill.

This *optional* stop provides a chance to examine the Empire Formation, which is not well exposed along the Going-to-the-Sun Road on the east side of the Park. This is the largest exposure of the Empire Formation along the road.

The Empire Formation was deposited in *transition*, when the predominantly tidal flat

Empire Formation.

environment of the underlying Grinnell Formation was yielding to the deeper water conditions of the overlying Helena (Siyeh) Formation. The Empire contains rocks similar to both these formations. Calcium and magnesium carbonate minerals were precipitating during Empire time. Also at that time, mud, silt, and some sand accumulated in diminishing amounts as the sea floor subsided.

The Empire Formation is a few hundred feet thick. It consists of gray to green argillite, siltite with dolomite cement, some quartzite, thin beds of red argillite, and a few thin beds of tan algal limestone and dolomite. A few layers in this outcrop appear rusty due to the weathering or oxidation of the iron sulfide mineral *pyrite* (FeS_2).

Proceeding to Stop 18, you wind down toward the bottom of U-shaped McDonald Creek valley. On your left, after you pass Logan Creek, are the steep, avalanche-tracked slopes of Mount Cannon. To your right is the ice-smoothed cliff of Glacier Wall. As you approach the west end of Glacier Wall, Heavens Peak comes into view.

Rocky Mountain sheep.

Eastbound Travelers
Distance from West Entrance to this stop
16.9 miles (27 km)

Next stop: Empire Formation
4.6 miles (7.4 km) east

Westbound Travelers
Distance from St. Mary Entrance to this stop
32.6 miles (52.2 km)

Next stop: Appekunny Formation
3.2 miles (5.1 km) west

Grinnell Formation

Optional

This optional stop is at a large parking area on the side of the road overlooking a picturesque bend in McDonald Creek.

This stop is *optional,* as it is somewhat repetitous of the Grinnell Formation at Stop 5. Here, however, the Grinnell contains some sedimentary features not present at Stop 5.

From the wall next to the parking area, you can see the crystal clear water of McDonald Creek meandering through and tumbling over the tilted red ledges of the Grinnell Formation. Notice that the layers

Cascading waters of McDonald Creek incise the colorful rocks of the Grinnell Formation at Red Rock Point.

of rock dip up-valley toward the east. This is because they are on the west limb of the *syncline* described at Stop 11.

If you walk down the trail from the parking area to McDonald Creek, you can see ripple marks and mudcracks formed when the argillite and siltite layers of the Grinnell Formation were being deposited on broad tidal flats. Gentle wave and current action caused the rippled surfaces on the mud and silt. Occasionally, during very low tides, the mud surfaces dried out, causing many-sided mudcracks to form, much the same as you see today in dried-up mud puddles. Additional layers of mud and silt were deposited on top of the mudcracked surface, thus preserving these delicate features in the geologic record.

Crossbedded quartzite bed.

In the roadcut opposite the parking area, where the photos on this page were taken, you can see thin beds of white, crossbedded quartzite (see photo above) and cross sections of sand-filled mudcracks (see photo below). The quartzite was deposited by

streams that drained the mainland and carried sheets of sand across the mud flats. At times, rapidly moving currents ripped up thin layers of dried mud and redeposited them in a jumble of flat mudchips, called mudchip breccias.

The bright red color of the Grinnell Formation is due to the presence of the red mineral *hematite* (Fe_2O_3). The hematite-bearing rocks were formed under oxidizing conditions on the tidal flat. The Grinnell contains a few green layers. One of these is just up the road from this stop. See the section on rock colors in the Appendix.

The massive mountain on the left as you approach Stop 19 is Mount Brown. On the right, numerous waterfalls tumble from *hanging valleys* between Stanton, Vaught, and McPartland Mountains (see foldout map).

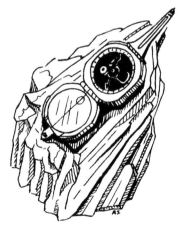

Geologist's compass.

Cross section of sand-filled mudcracks in argillite.

Eastbound Travelers
Distance from West Entrance to this stop
13.7 miles (22 km)

Next stop: Grinnell Formation
3.2 miles (5.1 km) east

Westbound Travelers
Distance from St. Mary Entrance to this stop
35.8 miles (57.3 km)

Next stop: Prichard Formation
1.4 miles (2.2 km) west

Appekunny Formation

Optional

This optional stop is a short walk from the parking area to McDonald Creek. Avoid the slippery, wet rocks near the stream.

The Appekunny Formation at this *optional* stop is also exposed at Stop 4 east of Logan Pass. The Appekunny was deposited in slightly deeper water here than at Stop 4, because the sea floor sloped westward during Appekunny time.

The Appekunny Formation *underlies* the Grinnell Formation. Remember that since

Greenish gray rocks of the Appekunny Formation flank the crystal clear water of McDonald Creek. (R.G. McGimsey photo.)

leaving Stop 13 at The Loop, you have been progressing downward through a sequence of older and older strata. The Appekunny Formation was deposited in quiet, fairly deep water and for the most part was undisturbed by waves and currents. It contrasts markedly, therefore, with the Grinnell Formation, which accumulated on a tidal flat. The Appekunny is composed of greenish gray siltite and argillite. Although these rocks contain some ripple marks and crossbedding, they lack features such as mudcracks that are produced only by periodic drying. The dominant features of the bedding are very thin laminations, which are well exposed in outcrops along McDonald Creek and in the roadcut across the road.

These rocks are gray to green because a lack of oxygen on the sea bottom kept the iron content of the sediments in a chemically *reduced* state (see Glossary). Much of this iron was later incorporated into the green, mica-like mineral *chlorite* which gives these rocks their color.

Circular depressions in the rocks along McDonald Creek, called *potholes*, are formed by the swirling action of pebbles carried by currents along the stream bed (see upper right photo). You will learn more about potholes at Stop 20.

Just down the road from Stop 19 you will pass "Moose Country," where you cross the thrust fault shown on the foldout map. This fault, which is not exposed near the road,

Small, well-formed pothole.

places the Prichard Formation over the Appekunny Formation, thus inverting the normal sequence.

Farther down the road, on your right, is Sacred Dancing Cascade, caused by stairstep ledges of the Prichard Formation in the bed of McDonald Creek. You will learn more about the Prichard at Stop 20.

Eastbound Travelers
Distance from West Entrance to this stop
12.3 miles (19.7 km)

Next stop: Appekunny Formation
1.4 miles (2.2 km) east

Westbound Travelers
Distance from St. Mary Entrance to this stop
37.2 miles (59.5 km)

Next stop: Lake McDonald Exhibit
2.7 miles (4.3 km) west

Prichard Formation

At this stop a trail begins at the west end of the parking area and leads to a footbridge across McDonald Creek. Please stay off the rocks next to the stream; they can be wet and slippery.

The Prichard Formation was deposited in deeper water than was any other formation in the Park. The dark gray to black argillite and siltite of this formation are characterized by very thin laminations that break into thin layers resembling *slate,* although technically it is not a true slate. The very thin laminations and abundant iron sulfide minerals (pyrite and pyrrhotite) dispersed through the rock indicate deep water and little oxygen—even deeper and poorer in oxygen than the Appekunny's

Cataracts and waterfalls *are formed by resistant ledges of the Prichard Formation along McDonald Creek about one mile (1.6 km) above the inlet of Lake McDonald.*

deposition environment. The rusty appearance of the rock along the creek is due to present-day weathering of the iron sulfide minerals.

Along Going-to-the-Sun Road the Prichard is the oldest formation on the west side of the Park, and the Altyn is the oldest on the east side. Both formations underlie the Appekunny (see the cross section on pages 10 and 11). However, although the Prichard and Altyn are equivalent in age, they were deposited in different settings in the Proterozoic sea. The Altyn was deposited in shallow water near shore, whereas the Prichard was deposited in much deeper

water some distance off-shore. This relationship reflects the westerly slope of the old sea bottom.

The large *potholes* in the rock downstream from the bridge were formed by the grinding action of pebbles and coarse sand which were whirled around and kept in motion by swift eddies in the stream. Such potholes can range in diameter from a few inches to many feet.

Notice the rugged steepness of the mountains at this stop. This topography contrasts sharply with the more gentle landscape you'll see at Stop 21.

Bull moose.

Eastbound Travelers
Distance from West Entrance to this stop
9.6 miles (15.5 km)

Next stop: Prichard Formation
2.7 miles (4.3 km) east

Westbound Travelers
Distance from St. Mary Entrance to this stop
39.9 miles (63.8 km)

This stop completes your Geology Tour.

Lake McDonald Exhibit

This stop is on the lake side of the road at the first full view of the lake west of Lake McDonald Lodge.

The depression now occupied by Lake McDonald was carved out of the McDonald Creek valley by a large glacier that flowed out of the mountains. Lateral moraines cap Howe Ridge across the lake and Snyder Ridge to the left, behind the trees. These moraines are made of rock debris that was carried on the glacier's flanks. The ridges

Serenely clear Lake McDonald, *fed by melting ice and snow, is impounded by low, tree-covered ridges.*

stand about 1,550 feet (473 m) above the lake level. Since the lake is 472 feet (144 m) deep, the combined figures indicate a minimum ice thickness at Lake McDonald of 2,022 feet (616 m). The ice reached this thickness about 20,000 years ago.

Note the difference in topographic relief and landforms at this stop as compared to Stop 20. There you were surrounded by high, rugged mountains made of resistant, ancient Proterozoic rocks. Here you are surrounded by low, tree-covered ridges and rounded hills of much younger, softer Tertiary rocks and unconsolidated glacial gravels. These ridges and hills impound Lake McDonald, which is fed by melting ice and snow.

AFTERWORD

We hope you have enjoyed this introduction to the geology of Glacier National Park. You have learned how the various sedimentary and igneous rocks were formed during Proterozoic time hundreds of millions of years ago. You have seen how massive collisions of the Earth's crustal plates shoved the Proterozoic rocks many miles to the east along the Lewis thrust fault. Finally, you have seen how mighty glaciers sculptured the magnificent peaks into rugged matterhorns and carved out the huge U-shaped valleys with their tributary hanging valleys. We hope this introduction has helped you gain new appreciation of these many natural wonders of the Park.

GLOSSARY

arête—a narrow, jagged, sharped-edged ridge or spur resulting from glacial erosion. See page 35.

argillite—a metamorphic rock of sedimentary origin composed of recrystallized clay minerals that still retains its sedimentary characteristics such as bedding, mudcracks, and mudchips.

basalt—a dark-colored, fine-grained volcanic rock composed chiefly of calcium-rich feldspar and other silicate minerals rich in iron and magnesium. Basalt is solidified lava.

bergschrund—a deep crevasse at the head of a mountain glacier that separates moving glacial ice from the snowfield at the head of the glacial valley. See page 24.

biotite—a black or dark-brown mineral of the mica group composed of potassium, magnesium, iron, aluminum, silicon, oxygen, and hydrogen.

breccia—a rock composed of angular and broken rock fragments that have been cemented together.

carbonaceous rock—a sedimentary rock containing an appreciable amount of organic material.

carbonate—a mineral or chemical compound composed of one or more metallic elements, usually calcium and magnesium, plus carbon and oxygen.

cement—mineral matter in the spaces between the individual grains of a consolidated sedimentary rock, binding the grains together as a rigid, coherent mass.

chlorite—a group of platy, usually greenish minerals, composed primarily of magnesium, iron, aluminum, silicon, oxygen, and hydrogen.

cirque—a steep-walled, amphitheater-like hollow on a mountainside, commonly at the head of a glacial valley, produced by the erosive activity of mountain glaciers. See pages 21 and 25.

Conophyton—a cone-shaped fossil form of algal colonies. See page 30.

Cretaceous—a geologic period and its corresponding rocks that cover the time span between 65 and 135 million years ago.

crevasse—a vertical fissure or crack in a glacier resulting from the differential movement of the ice. See page 24.

crossbedding—layers of sediment that were deposited at an angle to the major layers. See pages 17 and 48.

diorite—an igneous rock composed chiefly of the minerals feldspar and hornblende, with minor amounts of quartz, mica, and iron-oxide minerals.

dip—the angle that a surface, such as a bedding or fault plane, makes with the horizontal; that is, the angle of inclination of the plane.

dolomite—a mineral and a sedimentary rock composed of calcium and magnesium carbonate.

fault—a fracture in rock along which there has been movement, from a few centimeters to many kilometers. See pages 11 and 13.

feldspar—a group of rock-forming minerals composed primarily of the elements sodium, calcium, potassium, aluminum, silicon, and oxygen.

glacial flour—very fine rock powder that is formed when rocks embedded in the base and sides of a glacier abrade the underlying rocks.

glacier—a large mass of ice formed by the compaction and recrystallization of snow, moving slowly by internal flowage and slippage at the base downslope due to gravity. See page 24.

granite—a crystalline igneous or metamorphic rock composed chiefly of potassium- and sodium-rich feldspar, quartz, and mica.

hanging valley—a tributary glacial valley lying at a relatively high level on the steep side of a larger glacial valley.

hematite—a mineral composed of the elements iron and oxygen (Fe_2O_3).

horn—a sharply pointed, steep-sided, pyramidal mountain peak bounded by the intersecting walls of three or more cirques that have been cut back into a mountain by headward erosion of glaciers. See pages 26 and 33, and **matterhorn.**

hornblende—a common dark-colored mineral composed chiefly of calcium, sodium, magnesium, iron, aluminum, silicon, and oxygen.

igneous rock—a rock formed from molten or partly molten material. The word is derived from the Latin *ignis,* meaning fire.

isotope—one of two or more types of the same chemical element differing from one another by having different atomic weights.

landslide—a deposit formed by a general downslope movement of rock and soil material in response to gravity.

lateral moraine—a ridgelike accumulation of rock debris carried on, or deposited at or near, the side of a valley glacier.

limestone—a sedimentary rock composed mostly of the mineral calcite (calcium carbonate, $CaCO_3$).

magnetite—a black, strongly magnetic, opaque mineral composed primarily of iron and oxygen (Fe_3O_4).

marble—recrystallized limestone or dolomite composed mostly of the minerals calcite or dolomite.

matterhorn—a mountain that resembles the Matterhorn in the Pennine Alps. See **horn** and pages 26 and 33.

metamorphic rock—a rock derived from pre-existing rocks by mineralogical, chemical, and

Glossary (cont.)

structural changes in response to changes in temperature and pressure within the Earth's crust.

mica—a group of minerals that split into thin flakes, composed primarily of the elements potassium, sodium, calcium, magnesium, aluminum, silicon, oxygen, and hydrogen.

moraine—a ridge, mound, or other accumulation of unsorted and unstratified rock debris carried or deposited by a glacier. See page 25.

mudchip breccia—a sedimentary rock composed of angular chips of mud that have been cemented together. See page 23.

mudcracks—irregular fractures, often in a crudely polygonal pattern, formed by the shrinkage of clay, silt, or mud resulting from drying in air. See page 23.

mudstone—a sedimentary rock composed of approximately equal amounts of clay- and silt-sized material (consolidated mud).

oolite—a sedimentary rock composed mostly of ooliths. See page 42.

ooliths—small spherical objects that resemble small fish eggs. Most ooliths are made of calcite (calcium carbonate), but they can be made of other minerals. See page 42.

oxidation—a chemical process involving the combining of a substance with oxygen.

pothole—a smooth, bowl-shaped cavity formed in a stream bed by the grinding action of stones whirled around by eddying water currents. See page 50.

pyrite—a common, brass-yellow mineral composed of the elements iron and sulfur (FeS_2); also called fool's gold.

pyrrhotite—a common, reddish brown to brownish bronze mineral containing the elements iron and sulfur (FeS). It differs from pyrite in that it has a higher ratio of iron to sulfur.

quartz—a common mineral composed of silicon and oxygen (SiO_2).

quartzite—a sedimentary or metamorphic rock consisting chiefly of quartz grains, which is so completely hardened that the rock breaks across or through individual grains rather than around them. See **sandstone.**

radioactive decay—a spontaneous process in which an isotope (specific atomic weight) of one element loses particles from its nucleus to form an isotope of a new element. The rate of decay is constant, thus the amount of decay indicates elapsed time.

reduction—a chemical process operating in the absence of free oxygen, or the removal of oxygen from a substance.

ripple marks—wavy surface on the bedding plane of a sedimentary rock caused by the action of water currents, waves, or wind. See page 23.

sandstone—a sedimentary rock composed primarily of sand-sized quartz grains. It differs from quartzite in that it is not as well cemented;

therefore it breaks around individual grains rather than through them.

sedimentary rock—a rock resulting from the consolidation of sediment that was transported by water, wind, or ice.

sedimentation—the processes of physical or chemical deposition of sediment.

silicate—a mineral or chemical compound which has major components of silicon and oxygen.

sill—a tabular igneous rock body intruded generally parallel to the bedding or layering of the surrounding rock. See pages 31 and 43.

siltite—a slightly metamorphosed sedimentary rock composed mostly of silt-sized particles, in which most of the mineral grains have been recrystallized or altered by heat and pressure.

siltstone—a sedimentary rock formed by the consolidation of mostly silt-sized particles.

slate—a compact, fine-grained, metamorphic rock formed from such rocks as shale and volcanic ash. Slate usually splits along planes independent of the original bedding or laminations.

stromatolite—a fossil algae colony. The form commonly is composed of calcium carbonate and silt or mud trapped on the old surface of a sticky algal mat. Stromatolites show laminations in a variety of shapes that generally are convex upward and whose cross sections look like stacks of inverted cups or slices through a head of cabbage. See pages 17, 30, 40, and 44.

sulfide—a mineral or chemical compound composed of one or more metallic elements plus sulfur.

syncline—a downward fold of rock strata, the core of which contains stratigraphically younger rocks. The opposite form is an anticline. See page 36.

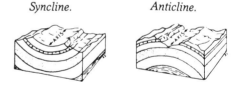

Syncline.   *Anticline.*

thrust fault—a low angle fault usually resulting in older rocks being superimposed over younger rocks. Such faults are usually the result of horizontal compression.

Thrust Fault.

transition zone—in sedimentary rocks, a rock sequence representing the change from one depositional environment to another.

APPENDIX

Brief Geologic History

Most of the rocks in Glacier National Park were deposited in and near a shallow sea during the middle Proterozoic hundreds of millions of years ago (see geologic time scale, page 8). These rocks were formed from sediments eroded from the North American continent over a period of about 800 million years.

This shallow sea occupied parts of present-day eastern Washington, the panhandle of Idaho, western Montana, and adjacent areas of Canada. More than 18,000 feet (5,500 m) of sediments slowly accumulated from highland source areas to the north, east, and south. The ever-increasing load forced the sea floor downward. Variations in downwarping on different parts of the sea floor, combined with changes in the amount and type of incoming sediment, resulted in the deposition of alternate layers of different kinds of sediment, including sand, silt, and limey mud. These materials were buried and compacted into sandstone, siltstone, shale, limestone, and dolomite.

As the great mass of sediment accumulated, moderate heat and pressure associated with deep burial caused mild metamorphism which converted the rocks to quartzite, siltite, argillite, and recrystallized limestone and dolomite. These rocks, however, have clearly retained most of their sedimentary characteristics.

Late in Proterozoic time, lavas erupted onto the sea floor in the area now included in the northern part of the Park. Still later, igneous rocks were injected into the sedimentary rocks and formed *sills* that parallel the layering in the rocks.

Sedimentary rocks that were deposited in Glacier National Park in Paleozoic time (see geologic time scale, page 8) have been removed by erosion. These rocks still exist in adjacent areas, but in Glacier Park the geologic record is missing for this time interval of perhaps 300 million years.

About 150 million years ago, a collision of the Earth's crustal plates on what then was the western edge of the North American continent elevated numerous mountain chains and formed the ancestral Rocky Mountains. Compressive forces persisted until about 60 million years ago and were great enough to produce mountains several hundred miles inland from the edge of the old continent. Ever-increasing stresses near the end of this great event shoved a huge rock wedge, several miles thick and several hundred miles wide, eastward more than 50 miles. In response to this enormous force, the sediments buckled into folds, and finally large masses of relatively stronger rocks were shoved over softer and more easily deformed rocks. Erosion through more millions of years stripped away the upper part of the original rock wedge and exposed the rocks and structures that we see in the Park today.

From the time of the plate collision to the present, rivers and streams have eroded and transported enormous amounts of sediment from the high ground to the oceans. By the end of the Tertiary Period, the mountains of Glacier National Park were fairly high but rounded, and the area contained broad stream valleys.

About 2 million years ago, the Earth's climate cooled world wide and the Ice Age began. Large ice sheets ebbed and flowed across much of the North American continent, and the high mountain valleys of the West filled with ice. When valley ice reached a thickness of perhaps 200 feet or so, it started to flow down the old stream valleys as glaciers. Rocks embedded in the ice acted as giant rasps, grinding away the bedrock of the valley floors, filing away the sides of the mountains, and producing the spectacular scenery of Glacier National Park. During relatively warm "interglacial" periods, the valleys were freed of ice, and rapidly flowing rivers cut deep gorges into the ice-carved rocks. The ice age persisted for almost 2 million years. The last of the huge glaciers disappeared from the Park about 12,000 years ago. Some scientists believe we are living today in a warm interglacial period and speculate that the glaciers might return.

Thus, the grandeur of Glacier National Park is the culmination of 60 million years of erosion by water and ice carving their way through a complex sequence of ancient sedimentary rocks. The geologic events that led to the formation of the rocks can be unscrambled by clues in the rocks themselves.

Rock Colors

The majestic scenery of Glacier National Park is enhanced by the intense and varied colors of the rocks. Shades of red, green, brown, and gray are due to disseminated iron-bearing minerals, or, in the case of the light gray rocks, to a lack of iron-bearing minerals. To a large extent, the colors reflect the environmental conditions under which the rocks were deposited and, to some extent, the conditions that occurred after they were deposited.

The red, maroon, and purple rocks owe their colors to the mineral hematite (Fe_2O_3), which was formed on the land surface or in shallow water by the interaction of iron with "free" oxygen from the atmosphere. Such conditions are referred to as an *oxidizing environment.* Hematite is a powerful coloring pigment. Amounts as low as three percent of the total rock are sufficient to impart a bright red, maroon, or purple hue to an entire rock mass. In Glacier Park, hematite resulted from the oxidation of other iron-bearing minerals carried in the channels and flood plains of rivers and deposited across tidal flats. Because hematite is chemically stable over a wide range of conditions, it has remained in the rocks since their formation.

The green rocks were formed in deeper water than were the red rocks, in an environment where oxygen from the atmosphere was less available for combination with iron. This setting is described as a *reducing environment.* Under such conditions, iron will combine with silica compounds to form iron silicate minerals. Then, upon low-grade metamorphism (minor increases in heat and pressure), the iron silicates convert to the green mineral *chlorite,* which is a hydrous iron-magnesium aluminum silicate. Abundant chlorite reflects a depositional environment offshore from the outer margin of the tidal flat. Alternating chlorite-bearing (green) and hematite-bearing (red) strata indicate fluctuations in sea level. It is interesting to note that the iron content of both red and green rocks is about the same.

With increasing heat and pressure, the hematite in the red beds and the chlorite in the green beds are converted to the dark-colored minerals magnetite and biotite. These minerals give the rocks a dark gray appearance. The biotite-rich Prichard Formation near Lake McDonald is an example.

Many of the limestones and dolomites in the Park are tan to buff on the surface of outcrops. On freshly broken surfaces, however, many of these rocks are gray, owing to traces of organic matter and iron. A few very light gray rocks contain almost no iron. Carbonate rocks with small amounts of iron, after long exposure to weathering, acquire thin tan to buff films of iron hydroxide on the surfaces of their outcrops.

Some of the rocks in the Park have a rusty appearance. These colors are due to weathering of iron sulfide minerals such as pyrite. In the oxidizing environment at and near the rock surface, the iron sulfide minerals readily convert to brown or yellow iron hydroxide and iron sulfate.

In summary, the colors in the rocks of Glacier National Park are caused by small amounts of various *iron minerals.* Indirectly, the colors and combinations of colors provide clues as to how the rocks were formed and what happened to them later.

Fossil Algae (Stromatolites)

Blue green algae that thrived in shallow parts of the Proterozoic sea played a significant role in the formation of the carbonate rocks of the Park. Stromatolites occur in many rocks of the Park but are confined mostly to the Altyn and Helena (Siyeh) Formations (see geologic cross section, pages 10 and 11.

The fossil forms of these ancient algae, called stromatolites, have shapes and internal structures very similar to the blue green algae that live in present-day seas. Modern algae grow where sunlight allows their metabolic processes to consume carbon dioxide from seawater and release oxygen as a waste product through the process of photosynthesis. There are two important results from this process: (1) oxygen released from the algae to the atmosphere provides an abundant supply of this life-supporting element; and (2) carbon dioxide removed from the seawater by the algae generates a chemical reaction that forms fine particles of calcium carbonate. The sticky, jellylike ooze secreted by the algae also traps fine sediment precipitated from the seawater or traps material washed into the sea.

Algae in the Proterozoic sea functioned in the same manner as their modern counterparts. They were a major factor in producing the oxygen-rich atmosphere that allowed development of other oxygen-consuming life forms on the Earth. Removal of carbon dioxide from seawater caused the formation of large quantities of calcium carbonate, which contributed to the great thicknesses of carbonate rocks in the Park. Stromatolites occur in several rock formations along the Going-to-the-Sun Road.

Rock Formations

Most of the rock formations discussed in this geologic guide were named for localities in the Park where the formations are well exposed. The names of these formations were proposed by Bailey Willis in 1902 and by M.O. Childers in 1963 and have been in popular use since those times. Mudge, in 1977, used the names Greyson, Spokane, Empire, and Helena from correlative rock units many miles to the south of Glacier Park, which were named by Walcott in 1899 and correspond for the most part to formations named by Willis. The names Appekunny and Grinnell were recently reinstated by the Geologic Names Committee of the U.S. Geological Survey. The boundaries of several of the formations, first named in 1902, have been changed by later investigations, as can be seen in the correlation chart opposite. Thereby this report is compatible with and bridges the older geological literature with the modern.

The following is a description of the Proterozoic rock formations, listed alphabetically, that can be seen along the Going-to-the-Sun Road. The correlation chart lists formations by geologic age. The formations have a wide range in thickness from place to place throughout the Park. The thicknesses listed below are typical of the formations near the road.

Altyn Formation—1,400 ft (427 m) thick (exposed); mostly limestone and dolomite, abundant quartz sand, some feldspar; light gray on fresh surfaces, weathers to light tan or cream color; abundant fossil algae (stromatolites).

Appekunny Formation—2,700 ft (823 m) thick; argillite and siltite; thick beds of quartzite near the base on the east side of the Park; gray to greenish gray, few thin beds of dark red to purplish red; thin, flat laminations, ripple marks, some layers have soft-sediment deformation.

Empire Formation—800 ft (244 m) thick; dolomitic siltite, argillite, and quartzite; gray to green plus a few thin beds of red argillite; weathers buff to light tan.

Grinnell Formation—1,420 ft (433 m) thick; argillite and siltite, numerous thin beds of quartzite; red to purplish red, few thin beds of green, quartzites commonly white; abundant ripple marks, mudcracks, crossbedding, and mudchip breccias.

Helena (Siyeh) Formation—2,500 ft (762 m) thick; primarily dolomite with some limestone; contains variable amounts of fine-grained quartz and clay minerals; medium to dark gray, weathers to various shades of tan; abundant fossil algae (stromatolites); upper part of formation is intruded by a dark grayish brown to black diorite sill forming a conspicuous layer.

Prichard Formation—4,000 ft (1220 m) thick (exposed); argillite and siltite; dark gray to black, rusty stains on weathered surfaces; very thin laminations, slatey appearance.

Shepard Formation—600 ft (183 m) thick (exposed); dolomitic siltite and dolomite, and a few beds of quartzite; gray and greenish gray, weathers yellowish gray to yellowish brown; contains beds of fossil algae (stromatolites).

Snowslip Formation—1,400 ft (427 m) thick; argillite, siltite, and minor amounts of quartzite, and carbonate-rich rocks; colors range from pale red to pale green with other shades of yellow, orange and light purple; few thin fossil algae (stromatolite) beds.

Marmot.

Correlation chart of the Proterozoic rocks in Glacier National Park, Montana.

GLACIER PARK Willis 1902	GLACIER PARK AND FLATHEAD REGION Ross (1959)	SOUTHWEST GLACIER PARK Childers (1963)	GLACIER PARK Mudge (1977)	GLACIER PARK WEST SIDE[1] (this book)	GLACIER PARK EAST SIDE[1] (this book)
		Unnamed rocks	McNamara Formation		
	Main Body (Missoula Group)	Red Plume Quartzite (Kintla Group)	Bonner Quartzite (Missoula Group)		
Kintla Argillite		Shields Formation	Mount Shields Formation		
Sheppard Quartzite	Shepard Formation	Shepard Formation	Shepard Formation	Shepard Formation	Shepard Formation
	Purcell Bst / Gca	Snowslip Formation (Belt Supergroup)	Purcell Bst / Snowslip Formation	Snowslip Formation	Snowslip Formation
Siyeh Limestone	Siyeh Limestone (Piegan Group)	Siyeh Formation	Helena Formation	Helena (Siyeh) Formation	Helena (Siyeh) Formation
			Empire Formation	Empire Formation	Empire Formation
Grinnell Argillite	Grinnell Argillite	Grinnell Formation	Spokane Formation	Grinnell Formation (Belt Supergroup)	Grinnell Formation (Belt Supergroup)
Appekunny Argillite	Appekunny Argillite (Ravalli Group)	Appekunny Formation	Greyson Formation (Ravalli Group)	Appekunny Formation	Appekunny Formation
		Thrust Fault	Altyn Formation		Altyn Formation
Altyn Limestone	Altyn Limestone			Prichard Formation	
Thrust Fault			Thrust Fault		Thrust Fault
				Base not exposed	

[1]Approximate boundary between the east and west sides of Glacier Park is the Continental Divide.

Abbreviations: Bst—Basalt; Gca—Green calcareous argillite.

61   Geology

REFERENCES CITED

Alden,W. C., and Stebinger, Eugene, 1913, Pre-Wisconsin glacial drift in the region of Glacier National Park, Montana: Geological Society of America Bulletin, v. 24, p. 529-572.

Campbell, M. R., 1914, The Glacier National Park: a popular guide to its geology and scenery: U.S. Geological Survey Bulletin 600, 54 p.

Childers, M. O., 1963, Structure and stratigraphy of the southwest Marias Pass area, Flathead County, Montana: Geological Society of America Bulletin, v. 74, no. 2, p. 141-164.

Fenton, C. L., and Fenton, M. A., 1931, Algae and algal beds in the Belt series of Glacier National Park: Journal of Geology, v. 39, p. 670-686.

Mudge, M. R., 1977, General geology of Glacier National Park and adjacent areas, Montana: Canadian Society Petroleum Geologists, v. 25, no. 4, p. 736-751.

Ross, C. P., 1959, Geology of Glacier National Park and the Flathead Region, northwestern Montana: U.S. Geological Survey Professional Paper 296. 125 p.

Walcott, C. D., 1899, Pre-Cambrian fossiliferous formations: Geological Society of America Bulletin, v. 10, p. 199-244.

Willis, Bailey, 1902, Stratigraphy and structure, Lewis and Livingston Ranges, Montana: Geological Society of America Bulletin, v. 13, p. 305-352.

Selected Additional Reading

Alt, D. D., and Hyndman, D. W., 1973, Rocks, Ice and Water—The geology of Waterton-Glacier Park: Mountain Press Publishing Company, 104 p.

Carrara, P. E., and McGimsey, R. G., 1981, The Late-Neoglacial histories of the Agassiz and Jackson glaciers, Glacier National Park, Montana: Arctic and Alpine Research, v. 13, no. 2, p. 183-196.

Harrison, J. E., 1972, Precambrian Belt Basin of Northwestern United States— its geometry, sedimentation and copper occurrences: Geological Society of America Bulletin, v. 83, p. 1215-1240.

Johnson, Arthur, 1980, Grinnell and Sperry Glaciers, Glacier National Park, Montana—A record of vanishing ice: U.S. Geological Survey Professional Paper 1180, 29 p.

Mudge, M. R., and Earhart, R. L., 1980, The Lewis Thrust Fault and related structures in the disturbed belt, northwestern Montana: U.S. Geological Survey Professional Paper 1174, 18 p.

Rezak, Richard, 1957, Stromatolites of the Belt Series in Glacier National Park and vicinity, Montana: U.S. Geological Survey Professional Paper 294-D, p. 127-154.

Ross, C. P., and Rezak, Richard, 1959, The rocks and fossils of Glacier National Park—the story of their origin and history: U.S. Geological Survey Professional Paper 294-K, p. 401-439.

Shaded Relief, Oblique View Geologic Map, Vicinity of Going-to-the-Sun-Road, Glacier National Park, Montana

By:
Arthur L. Isom: shaded-relief art and drafting
Robert L. Earhart, Omer B. Raup, and James W. Whipple: geology
Drexel A. Brumley and Stafford G. Binder: computer-generated base map

The production of this map began with aerial photography taken from an elevation of 40,000 feet. The photography allowed the area to be viewed stereoscopically (in three dimensions) and made possible the horizontal and vertical measurements of the geographic features. Eight stereomodels were scanned on a digital photogrammetric instrument attached to a magnetic tape drive. Elevations were collected and recorded onto tape every 50 meters along profiles 100 meters apart, resulting in a total of 570,000 data points. These data were reduced to 36,000 location and elevation points by a computer program which compiled a three-dimensional contour perspective model in the computer's memory. The model was oriented so that the resulting map would be viewed from the south, would have a 30-degree tilt, and have a 2.6-times vertical exaggeration. These conditions were selected to give maximum visibility of Going-to-the-Sun Road, minimum concealment of terrain, and realism of geographic features. The model was transferred to magnetic tape from the computer's memory, entered into and drawn by a plotter.

This air-brush, shaded-relief version of the map was made using the three-dimensional oblique contour map as a base, along with oblique aerial photographs and standard topographic maps. The geology was added from data obtained by field mapping and from oblique color aerial photographs.

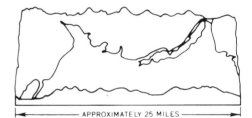

APPROXIMATELY 25 MILES

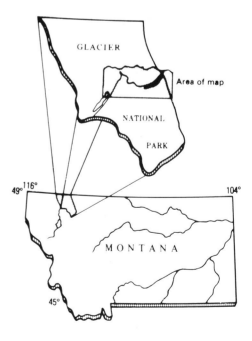

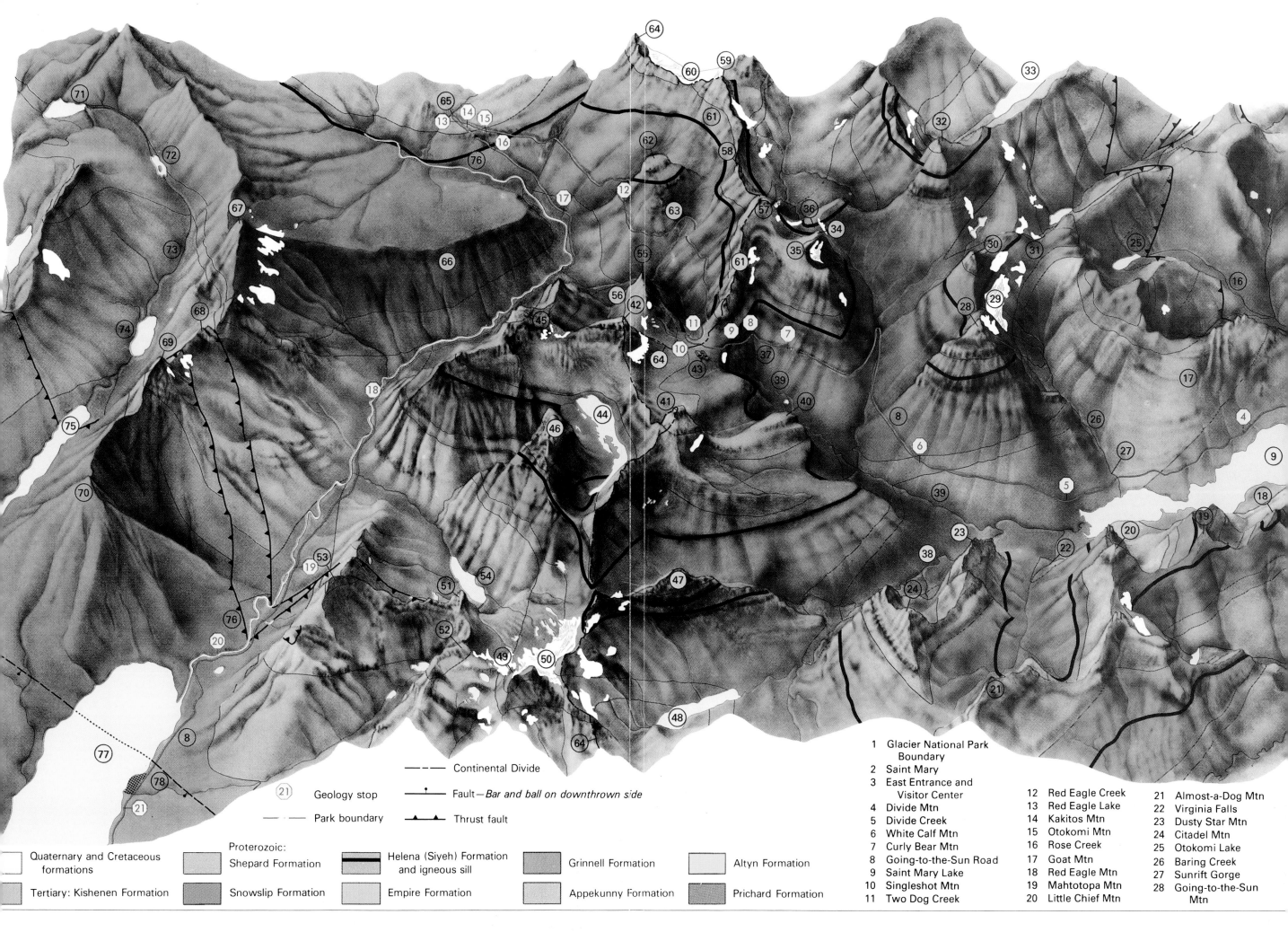

Legend / Key:

--- — Continental Divide

(21) Geology stop

--- — Park boundary

⊢—⊢ Fault—Bar and ball on downthrown side

▲▲ Thrust fault

1 Glacier National Park Boundary
2 Saint Mary
3 East Entrance and Visitor Center
4 Divide Mtn
5 Divide Creek
6 White Calf Mtn
7 Curly Bear Mtn
8 Going-to-the-Sun Road
9 Saint Mary Lake
10 Singleshot Mtn
11 Two Dog Creek

12 Red Eagle Creek
13 Red Eagle Lake
14 Kakitos Mtn
15 Otokomi Mtn
16 Rose Creek
17 Goat Mtn
18 Red Eagle Mtn
19 Mahtotopa Mtn
20 Little Chief Mtn

21 Almost-a-Dog Mtn
22 Virginia Falls
23 Dusty Star Mtn
24 Citadel Mtn
25 Otokomi Lake
26 Baring Creek
27 Sunrift Gorge
28 Going-to-the-Sun Mtn

Formations:

☐ Quaternary and Cretaceous formations

☐ Tertiary: Kishenen Formation

Proterozoic:

☐ Shepard Formation

☐ Snowslip Formation

▬ Helena (Siyeh) Formation and igneous sill

☐ Empire Formation

☐ Grinnell Formation

☐ Appekunny Formation

☐ Altyn Formation

☐ Prichard Formation

LEWIS THRUST FAULT

LEWIS THRUST FAULT

N

89